The Fla

by Katherine Scraper

I need to know these words.

flag

pole

stars

stripes

Look at the flag.
The flag has stars.

Look at the flag.
The flag has stripes.

Look at the flag.
The flag has red stripes.

Look at the flag.
The flag has white stripes.

Look at the flag.
The flag has white stars.

Look at the flag.

The flag has a pole.

Look at the flag!